ALL ABOUT INSECTS

ALL ABOUT BEES

by Karen Latchana Kenney

pogo

Ideas for Parents and Teachers

Pogo Books let children practice reading informational text while introducing them to nonfiction features such as headings, labels, sidebars, maps, and diagrams, as well as a table of contents, glossary, and index.

Carefully leveled text with a strong photo match offers early fluent readers the support they need to succeed.

Before Reading

- "Walk" through the book and point out the various nonfiction features. Ask the student what purpose each feature serves.
- Look at the glossary together. Read and discuss the words.

Read the Book

- Have the child read the book independently.
- Invite him or her to list questions that arise from reading.

After Reading

- Discuss the child's questions. Talk about how he or she might find answers to those questions.
- Prompt the child to think more. Ask: Have you ever seen a bee? What did it look like, and what was it doing?

Pogo Books are published by Jump!
5357 Penn Avenue South
Minneapolis, MN 55419
www.jumplibrary.com

Library of Congress Cataloging-in-Publication Data

Names: Kenney, Karen Latchana, author.
Title: All about bees / by Karen Latchana Kenney.
Description: Minneapolis, MN: Jump!, Inc., [2024]
Series: All about insects | Includes index.
Audience: Ages 7-10
Identifiers: LCCN 2022045746 (print)
LCCN 2022045747 (ebook)
ISBN 9798885244244 (hardcover)
ISBN 9798885244251 (paperback)
ISBN 9798885244268 (ebook)
Subjects: LCSH: Bees—Juvenile literature.
Classification: LCC QL565.2 .K455 2024 (print)
LCC QL565.2 (ebook)
DDC 595.79/9—dc23/eng/20221003
LC record available at https://lccn.loc.gov/2022045746
LC ebook record available at https://lccn.loc.gov/2022045747

Editor: Jenna Gleisner
Designer: Emma Almgren-Bersie

Photo Credits: stockfotocz/iStock, cover; Kuttelvaserova Stuchelova/Shutterstock, 1, 9; Tsekhmister/iStock, 3; Maciej Olszewski/Alamy, 4; Darren Brode/Shutterstock, 5; Angelshot/Dreamstime, 6-7tl; Megan Kobe/iStock, 6-7tr; Inventori/iStock, 6-7bl; ElementalImaging/iStock, 6-7br; RooM the Agency/Alamy, 8; Frank Reiser/Shutterstock, 10-11; mady70/iStock, 12-13; Yuttana Joe/Shutterstock, 14-15; Yue_/iStock, 16; a8096b40_190/iStock, 17; Toltek/iStock, 18-19; blickwinkel/Alamy, 20-21; Verastuchelova/Dreamstime, 23.

Printed in the United States of America at Corporate Graphics in North Mankato, Minnesota.

TABLE OF CONTENTS

CHAPTER 1

HELLO, BEE!

Two large black eyes watch. **Antennas** feel and smell. A long, hollow tongue called a proboscis sucks **nectar**. What is this **insect**? It is a bumblebee! More than 20,000 kinds of bees buzz around the world. Many are yellow and black.

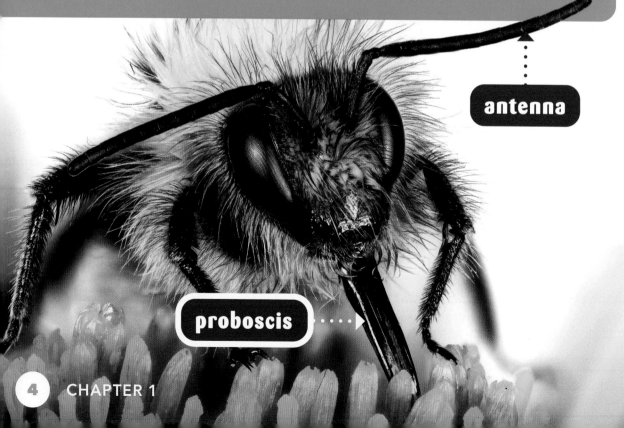

antenna

proboscis

abdomen

thorax

head

Some sweat bees are bright green or
blue. All bees fly with two sets of wings.
Each has three body sections: a head,
a thorax, and an abdomen. They have
jaws and six legs. They have hairs, too.

Bees start as eggs. They hatch as **larvae**. They look like white worms. They eat and grow.

When they are big enough, they form **cocoons**. Other bees may seal them inside wax or mud cells. In their cocoons, they are **pupae**. When they come out, they are adults.

egg ·····▶

larva ·····▶

pupa ·····▶

adult

CHAPTER 2

IN THE HIVE

Different kinds of bees live in different areas of the world. The only place bees do not live is Antarctica. Many bees live in prairies and forests. Cactus bees live in the desert.

cactus bee

Yellow and black honeybees fly in and out of a hollow tree. Their **hive** is inside. Honeybees are **social** bees.

Social bees live in large **colonies**. More than 60,000 bees can live in a hive! The females have stingers. They sting **predators** such as bears and skunks.

Beestings hurt! Why? **Glands** connect to a bee's stinger. The glands pump **venom** into the bee's enemy.

DID YOU KNOW?

Male social bees don't have stingers. Why? They don't protect the hive, so they don't need them.

stinger

queen

cell

Honeybees find spaces to build their hives. The bees make wax. They form the wax into cells.

Cells can have different uses. Some hold food. The queen lays eggs in others.

TAKE A LOOK!

What are the parts of a social beehive? Take a look!

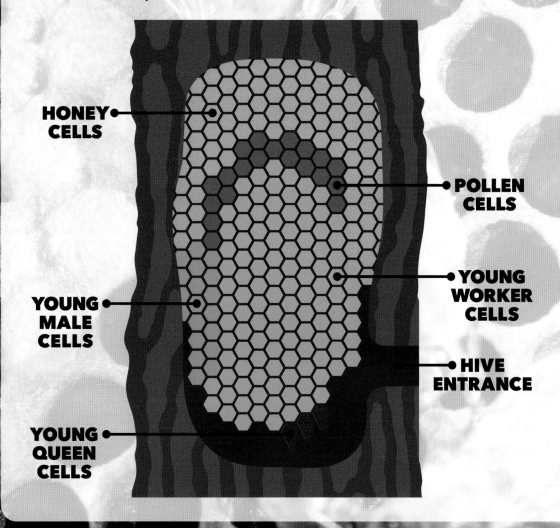

HONEY CELLS

POLLEN CELLS

YOUNG WORKER CELLS

YOUNG MALE CELLS

HIVE ENTRANCE

YOUNG QUEEN CELLS

carpenter bee

Most bees are solitary. This means they live alone. They make nests in the ground or in plants. They dig tunnels or build cells. Carpenter bees are one kind of solitary bee. They nest in plant stems.

Solitary bees do not sting. Why? They leave their nests after laying eggs. They do not protect them.

DID YOU KNOW?

Some bees do not make nests. They steal other bees' nests! The cuckoo bee lays its egg in another bee's nest. Its larva hatches first. Then, it eats the food meant for the other bee's larvae.

CHAPTER 3

POLLEN SPREADERS

Bees collect food from flowers. Bright flower petals **attract** them. A bee sucks nectar with its proboscis. Nectar gives the bee energy.

pollen

Pollen sticks to the bee's hairs. Pollen has protein and fat. Some bees collect it on their legs.

Social worker bees bring food back to the hive. They give it to other worker bees. They put it in cells. The nectar turns into honey. Pollen goes into other cells. Both become food for the colony.

Solitary bees make balls of pollen and nectar. These go next to each egg. Larvae eat the balls as they grow.

honey cells

pollen cells

As bees fly from flower to flower, they **pollinate** the plants. Pollen helps plants make seeds. Then, new plants grow.

Bees keep our planet alive and healthy. Have you seen bees?

ACTIVITIES & TOOLS

BUILD A BEE HOME

Build a bee home for solitary bees with this fun activity!

What You Need:

- metal can, such as an empty coffee can
- black or brown paint
- paintbrush
- paper
- scissors
- paper straws or hollow plant stems
- string

❶ Bees nest in dark places. Paint your metal can black or brown. Let the can dry on paper for a few hours.

❷ Fill the can with straws or plant stems. They should fit tightly in the can. Make sure the open ends face the open part of the can.

❸ Trim the straws or plant stems to fit inside the can.

❹ Tie string around the round part of the can. Leave a long end.

❺ Find a good spot for the bee home. Put it in a place that is sheltered from rain. Tie the long end of the string around a tree branch or a post.

❻ Wait and watch. If a straw or stem is sealed, a bee made a nest in it!

GLOSSARY

antennas: Feelers on the head of an insect.

attract: To get something's interest.

cocoons: Coverings made by larvae or other small insects to protect themselves or their eggs.

colonies: Large groups of insects that live together.

glands: Organs in the body that produce or release chemicals.

hive: A home that is made by bees and filled with wax cells.

insect: A small animal with three pairs of legs, one or two pairs of wings, and three main body parts.

larvae: Insects in the stage of growth between eggs and pupae.

nectar: A sweet liquid made by flowers.

pollen: Tiny yellow grains in flowers that plants need to make seeds.

pollinate: To carry pollen from flower to flower, allowing plants to form seeds.

predators: Animals that hunt other animals for food.

pupae: Insects in the stage of growth between larvae and adults.

social: Living in colonies or groups rather than alone.

venom: A poisonous liquid.

INDEX

TO LEARN MORE

Finding more information is as easy as 1, 2, 3.

❶ Go to www.factsurfer.com

❷ Enter "bees" into the search box.

❸ Choose your book to see a list of websites.

FACT SURFER